Books are to be returned on or before
the last date below.

KT-502-419

- 6 JAN 2011

INNOVATORS

John Lasseter

Pixar Animator

Other titles in the Innovators series include:

INNOVATORS

John Lasseter
Pixar Animator

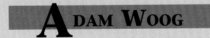

ADAM **W**OOG

KIDHAVEN PRESS
A part of Gale, Cengage Learning

GALE
CENGAGE Learning™

Detroit • New York • San Francisco • New Haven, Conn • Waterville, Maine • London

GALE
CENGAGE Learning™

Dedication
For Karen, who believed me when I said that watching every Pixar movie was just research, and for Leah, who has enjoyed them with us over the years.

LIBRARY OF CONGRESS CATALOGING-IN-PUBLICATION DATA

Woog, Adam, 1953-
  John Lasseter : Pixar animator / by Adam Woog.
    p. cm. — (Innovators)
  Includes bibliographical references and index.
  ISBN 978-0-7377-4080-6 (hbk.)
  1. Lasseter, John—Juvenile literature. 2. Motion picture producers and directors— United States—Biography—Juvenile literature. 3. Pixar (Firm)—Juvenile literature. I. Title.
    PN1998.3.L3925W66 2009
    791.4302'33092—dc22
    [B]

                                                                2008022002

KidHaven Press
27500 Drake Rd.
Farmington Hills, MI 48331

ISBN-13: 978-0-7377-4080-6
ISBN-10: 0-7377-4080-9

Printed in the United States of America
1 2 3 4 5 6 7 13 12 11 10 09

CONTENTS

Meet Mr. Pixar

One weekend, John Lasseter and his wife Nancy took their five sons to the movies. John is the creative genius behind Pixar Animation Studios. Pixar is the top studio in the world making computer-animated movies. Its hits include *Toy Story, A Bug's Life, Toy Story 2, Monsters, Inc., Finding Nemo, The Incredibles, Cars*, and *Ratatouille*.

Lasseter loves going to the movies with his kids, but this one was boring. At one point, his youngest son, who was about six, turned to Lasseter and asked him how many letters were in his name. Lasseter laughed and realized that his son had lost interest in the movie. His mind was wandering.

That was an important lesson for Lasseter. It brought home the importance of keeping movies interesting—to kids and adults. He promised himself, "If ever a child anywhere in the world leans over to their daddy during one of my movies and asks, 'How many letters are in my name?' I'll quit."[1]

The Popular Favorite

Lasseter has taken that lesson to heart. He works hard to make sure that every Pixar movie has amazing, eye-popping graphics—and much more. He makes sure it also has a strong story, delightful characters, and powerful emotions. He considers all of these important parts of a successful movie.

John Lasseter shows off one of his two Academy Awards for special achievement in animation.

This combination is definitely a winner. Each of Lasseter's feature films has been a smash success. Each one has set new attendance records with audiences around the world.

Pixar movies are not just popular with audiences, either. Critics routinely praise them for their intelligence, entertainment, and spirit. The films have also won many awards. Among these are many Oscar nominations and wins. Lasseter has personally won two Oscars so far, one for animated short film (*Tin Toy*) and one for special achievement (*Toy Story*).

No Equal

Before Pixar's skyrocketing arrival on the movie scene, animation had fallen in popularity. However, the smash successes of Lasseter's movies made animation wildly popular. Many new animated movies are now being made. In this way, Lasseter has changed how Hollywood works.

This influence gives Lasseter a lot of impact in the world of moviemaking. Today, he is widely recognized as the single most respected and important person in animation. He is also one of the most powerful people in Hollywood—if not the most powerful of all.

Lasseter's achievements stand head and shoulders above those of other computer animators. The company he helped found has many competitors, but no equal. Film critic Moira Macdonald comments, "In the world of animated movies, there's Pixar . . . and then there's everyone else."[2]

Pixar and Disney

In its creativity and success rate, Pixar has overtaken even the studio started by Walt Disney. Disney was the genius whose creations of Mickey Mouse and other world-famous characters changed animation forever. But about ten years ago the Disney Corporation's once-great animation department fell on hard times, and its movies were flopping.

So recently Disney bought Pixar. The giant company gave Lasseter creative control over both Pixar and Disney's animation studios. The executives at Disney hope that Lasseter's magic touch can revive their animation department to its former glory.

This new job is fitting for Lasseter, because he is widely seen as the heir to the throne of Walt Disney himself. The new job is also a great honor to Lasseter personally, because all his life he has wanted to work at the famous Walt Disney Studios. It was his fondest and highest dream.

Not bad for such a nice guy. By all accounts, Lasseter is the same friendly, toy-loving, enthusiastic "big kid" he always has been. He almost always wears jeans and bright Hawaiian shirts, even to formal occasions. This casual personal style—and his undying love for cartoons—began when he was very young.

CHAPTER 1

The Early Years

John Alan Lasseter was a bit of a surprise when he was born. He was a twin. His mother did not know she was having twins until just before giving birth to them.

John was born just six minutes after his sister, Joanne. John's father later joked that John was the family's "bonus baby."

Loving Cartoons

John was born in Hollywood, California, on January 12, 1957. He, Joanne, and their older brother Jim grew up in nearby Whittier. Their father managed the parts department at a Chevrolet dealership. Their mother taught high school art in nearby Bell Gardens.

When he was a boy, John liked to do many things. For instance, he liked to play with Hot Wheels cars. But his favorite thing was watching cartoons.

Home video and 24-hour cartoon channels did not yet exist. John could only see cartoons on Saturday mornings and

After graduating from college in 1979, John realized his
lifelong dream when he began working at Walt Disney's
Animation Division.

after school—so he was always at home at those times. He remembers, "Even though you couldn't get me out of bed on a weekday, come Saturday morning I was up at 6:30 waiting . . . for the cartoons to begin. I'd have my bowl of cereal and sit really close to the TV and watch all the cartoons until the sports came on."[3]

Drawing

John also began drawing at an early age. Since his mother taught art, materials were always around the house. John got his first award at age five, when he won $15 from the Model Grocery Market for a crayon drawing of the Headless Horseman.

As he grew older, John continued to draw and watch cartoons. He says he did this every day after class, even in high school and even though he knew it was not cool.

As a teen, John read a book that made a big impression. *The Art of Animation*, by Bob Thomas, was a behind-the-scenes look at the making of Disney's *Sleeping Beauty*. After reading it, he was surprised to realize that making cartoons could be a real job.

Disney's Apprentice

Disney movies always fascinated John, and he saw every one that he could. He wrote to the studio, saying that he wanted to become an animator. He got an encouraging letter back. It told John that he should study art and learn figure drawing, design, and color. Then he could learn animation while working for Disney, because no college taught it. The letter also invited John to tour Walt Disney Animation Studios, which was one of the most exciting things he had ever done.

Then, during John's senior year of high school, the Disney company sent a letter to several promising young artists, including John. The letter mentioned a new program at the California Institute of the Arts in nearby Valencia. It was going to be for people interested in becoming animators. The teachers were going to be former Disney artists.

Walt Disney Studios thought John could do very well in the new program. So the studio gave him a scholarship after he graduated from high school. John became the second student chosen for the new program.

Of course, John was very excited. He learned many skills there from people he considered masters. They were the artists who had taken animation from its infancy to a high level. Now they were passing their knowledge on to John and his classmates.

John spent his summers working as an operator on Disneyland's Jungle Cruise ride, shown here in 1955.

Summer Jobs

While still at art school, John worked at Disneyland during his summer vacations. He was a sweeper at Tomorrowland and then a ride operator on the Jungle Cruise. The Jungle Cruise is one of the oldest and most popular theme rides at Disneyland. It is an exciting ride through a pretend jungle.

Ride operators on the Jungle Cruise have a script to follow, but they are also allowed to make up their own jokes. With lots of corny jokes and an audience that could not leave, John found that even the worst joke is funny—if it is told well. He says that this job helped cure his shyness and develop his love of entertaining.

During this period of his life, another important thing happened to John. He saw *Star Wars*. He was amazed at how the movie captured the imaginations of everyone—young, old, and families. That was what John wanted to do—tell stories that were exciting, fun, and entertaining to everyone.

John graduated from college in 1979 and was hired as an animator at Walt Disney Animation Studios. At first it seemed like a dream come true. All he had ever wanted to do was work at Disney.

"This Is the Future!"

However, the reality was disappointing. To Lasseter, it seemed that the fun was gone at Disney. The people who ran the studio then were only interested in making money. Still, Lasseter stayed for five years. Among the films he worked on were *The Fox and the Hound* and *Mickey's Christmas Carol*.

While at Disney, Lasseter saw something new and exciting: computer animation. At the time, this was a brand-new way to

Lasseter's first big project for Disney was working on the animated feature *The Fox and the Hound*, pictured.

create animation, using computers instead of handmade drawings. The images Lasseter saw were being made for an upcoming science-fiction movie called *Tron*.

Lasseter saw that computer animation could help artists create some amazing new things, because they could draw a realistic, three-dimensional world. He remembers, "It absolutely blew me away! A little door in my mind opened up. I looked at it and said, 'This is it! This is the future!'"[4]

Fired . . .

In 1981 Lasseter and a friend created a half-minute film with hand-drawn characters and a computer-generated background.

Ed Catmull, the president of Pixar, poses at the studio in 2004. Catmull hired Lasseter after he was fired from Disney.

They hoped to show off the amazing things that could be created with computers. But the Disney executives were not interested. They only wanted to use computers if they could make regular animation cheaper.

Lasseter kept trying. He wanted approval to make a full-length computer-generated movie based on a book called *The Brave Little Toaster*. But John made some Disney executives angry. They thought he was sneakily going behind their backs to try to get his movie made.

As a result, Lasseter was fired. Of course, he was very upset. All his life, working at Disney had been his dream. He was ashamed to tell people he had been fired.

But there was a silver lining. While planning *The Brave Little Toaster*, Lasseter had met many people working in computer graphics. Among them was Ed Catmull. He worked for a division of Lucasfilm, the film company started by *Star Wars* creator George Lucas.

In 1983, soon after he was fired, Lasseter met Catmull again at a conference. By the end of the day, Catmull had hired Lasseter for a project. They created a computer animated short called *The Adventures of André and Wally B.*

. . . and Hired

To work on the project, Lasseter moved to the San Francisco Bay Area, where Lucasfilm was located. His job was supposed to last only one month, but he stayed at Lucasfilm longer. He was there in 1986 when Steve Jobs entered the scene.

Jobs was the cofounder and chairman of Apple Computer. He bought Lucasfilm's computer graphics division. Jobs made it independent and renamed it Pixar. The next phase of Lasseter's life was about to begin.

CHAPTER 2

Building Pixar

Lasseter had a lot of freedom in the new company. He could create almost any story he wanted. For example, in 1986 he wrote and directed *Luxo Jr.*, the first short cartoon produced by Pixar as an independent company.

Luxo Jr. was only two and a half minutes long, but it was memorable. It starred an active little lamp and its weary parent. Lasseter was inspired when he walked past a furniture store one day and noticed a lamp in the window. He got the idea to make the lamp come to life.

Lasseter was honored when *Luxo Jr.* was nominated for an Oscar in the Best Short Film, Animated category. It did not win, but Lasseter and his team had learned a lot while making it. Their next short was *Tin Toy*, about a destructive baby and a nervous windup toy. This time, their work did win an Oscar. It was the first film made completely with computers, not traditional animation, to win this special award.

A Turning Point

These two short films are modest by today's standards. At the time, though, they were far more advanced than anything else people had seen. They still delight audiences today.

The early Pixar shorts were important in several ways. They proved that computer animation could be a serious creative tool, not just a cool novelty. Also, their success helped make Pixar the top company in the growing computer-animation business.

Furthermore, they marked a turning point in Lasseter's career. They cemented his reputation as the single most important man in computer animation. Catmull, a key member of the

Lasseter's talent in animation led the way for animators like these men. They are scanning a plane for computer animation.

Pixar team, comments, "Don't forget how visionary John was as an artist back then. Remember, it was only 1981 when the IBM PC first came out. Back then no one really knew what to do with them."[5]

A Full-Length Movie Takes Shape

Over the next decade, Pixar continued to grow. When Jobs, the head of Apple, bought it, only about 45 people worked there. But as it became successful, the company grew. By 2001, Pixar had more than 600 employees, so it moved to a huge new campus

Apple Computer cofounder Steve Jobs bought Pixar in the late 1980s. He quickly hired Lasseter to work on short animated films.

in Emeryville, California. The atmosphere there was casual and fun-loving. Employees played badminton or swam during breaks and used scooters to zip between meetings.

Meanwhile, Pixar made about one short film a year. It also made commercials for such clients as Tropicana, Listerine, Lifesavers, the California Lottery, Volkswagen, and Pillsbury. With each project, Lasseter and his crew learned more and got better at their craft. Their goal was to learn enough to make a full-length feature film.

During this time, a new group of people gained control over Walt Disney Studios. They liked Lasseter's work. In fact, they wanted him to come work for Disney again.

This time, however, Lasseter said no, because he liked working at Pixar. He knew he had the best computer-animation group in the world. But he also wanted to do something with Disney. He knew that big Disney had the money to help little Pixar make a full-length movie.

The partnership between the two studios started in 1991. Disney agreed to give $26 million to Pixar. In return, Pixar agreed to produce at least three feature films for Disney. Lasseter and his group started work right away on the world's first completely computer-animated feature film.

Toy Story

As millions of movie fans know, this was *Toy Story*. Part of the inspiration for its plot came from *Tin Toy*. Lasseter had enjoyed how that short film had looked at life from a toy's point of view. Another inspiration was his love of "buddy" movies. He wanted to tell a story about two characters who dislike each other at first but come to love and respect each other.

Action figure Buzz Lightyear, left, and Woody, the friendly cowboy, appear in *Toy Story*, the world's first computer-animated feature film.

So Lasseter and three writers created a story about toys that compete for the attention of their owner. Its stars were Woody, a friendly cowboy doll, and Buzz Lightyear, a high-energy, action-hero toy. Their friends included Mr. Potatohead, Slinky Dog, and other classic toys.

Toy Story was a huge hit. Audiences loved it so much that the film made more money than any other in 1995. Movie critics loved it, too, calling it one of the best films of the year.

There were several reasons for Toy Story's success. First of all, the computer graphics were great. Also, talented actors such as Tom Hanks and Tim Allen, who provided the voices for the movie, added a lot. But most important were the movie's exciting plot and humanlike personalities. Lasseter says, "You cannot base a whole movie on just the [graphics] alone. It has to be the story and the characters."[6]

More Blockbusters

Toy Story set a high standard for computer animation. The movie industry honored it with four Oscar nominations, and Lasseter received a Special Achievement Oscar. It also changed what Hollywood studios thought about animated features. Suddenly, animation became big business.

For Lasseter, the challenge was to follow Toy Story with even better movies. He succeeded. All of Pixar's next movies were huge critical and box-office successes. Lasseter was closely involved with all of them as a director and/or producer.

Lasseter poses with his wife Nancy while holding his Golden Globe Award for the 2006 movie *Cars*.

Lasseter's second movie was *A Bug's Life*, which came out in 1998. It starred an ant named Flik. Flik has to save his colony from greedy grasshoppers by pulling together a group of misfit insects. Again, it was nominated for an Oscar.

The next year, 1999, Lasseter and his team released a sequel to *Toy Story*. In *Toy Story 2*, Buzz and the other toys have to rescue Woody after a toy collector steals him. Lasseter says he usually does not like sequels, because they are often not as good as the original. However, in this case he had a good story and characters that he already knew were strong.

And More Blockbusters

More smash hits followed: *Monsters, Inc.* in 2001, *Finding Nemo* in 2003, *The Incredibles* in 2004, *Cars* in 2006, and *Ratatouille* in 2007. With John as creative guide, all of them were wildly successful. They set new box-office records and collected many awards, including Best Animated Feature Oscars for *Finding Nemo* and *The Incredibles*.

Cars was the first movie in several years that Lasseter directed himself. He chose it, in part, because he loves cars. The characters in the movie reminded him of the Hot Wheels cars he had played with as a kid.

Each of these movies, including *Cars*, taught Lasseter several lessons. Of course he learned how to make better and better movies. More important, however, he learned valuable lessons about life.

CHAPTER 3

Lessons from Pixar

O ver the years, Lasseter has learned important lessons about what it takes to make a good movie. He began learning these lessons as a kid watching cartoons, especially those by his hero, Walt Disney. He has refined those ideas through years of making his own movies. Lasseter says he learns something new every time he makes a movie.

One of the most important lessons Lasseter has learned is that no movie can survive on special effects alone. Movies that rely only on flashy pictures will soon be forgotten. But strong stories, themes, and characters create classics.

Also, Lasseter has learned to put real emotions into his movies. His movies recognize that life is often funny, but sometimes it is also sad. He says, "We love to laugh, but I also believe what Walt Disney said: 'For every laugh there should be a tear.'"[7]

No Boredom Allowed

Another lesson Lasseter has learned is that a strong theme can teach audiences something about life. For example, a theme in many Pixar movies is the importance of friendship. But Lasseter has learned that a movie can teach something while also being entertaining and exciting. It does not have to be a boring lecture.

In fact, Lasseter says the most important part of his job is simply to entertain. He says, "If you walk out with a smile on your face, saying, 'That was a good movie, I didn't waste my time,' that to me is success."[8]

The Nancy Factor

Lasseter has learned some lessons about moviemaking from his wife Nancy, herself a former animation engineer. For example, she makes sure that his movies appeal to as many people as possible. This has become known at Pixar as the Nancy Factor.

John says that Nancy always reminds him that his audience is made up of adults as well as kids. These grown-ups include both parents and adults without kids. The Nancy Factor helps make sure that none of these adults will be bored. There will always be plenty of interesting things in a Pixar movie, so even grown-ups who have watched the movie many times with their kids can find something to enjoy.

For one thing, the realism of the animation fascinates adults, such as the lifelike quality of the toys and people in *Toy Story*. Another example is that grown-ups understand a lot of the humorous touches that kids might not get, such as the name of the restaurant in *Monsters, Inc.* Harryhausen's is named in honor of Ray Harryhausen, a pioneer of movie special effects.

Her husband John calls Nancy Lasseter's opinion the Nancy Factor. She helps ensure that John's movies appeal to adults as well as children.

The Nancy Factor also makes sure that the themes and details of Pixar movies are easy for everyone to enjoy. For instance, John loves cars, so of course he was excited about making *Cars* and putting in lots of details about racing. But Nancy reminded him that not everyone shares the same passion. The Nancy Factor made sure that *Cars* was interesting even for people who do not love racing.

An Idea from Life

Lasseter often gets ideas for movies from his own life. For example, he thought of the plot for *Toy Story 2* when his sons wanted to play with his valuable toy collection. This collection includes such rare items as a Woody doll signed by Tom Hanks.

At first Lasseter wanted to protect his valuable toys. But then he had second thoughts. He recalls, "I asked myself, 'John, what did you learn from *Toy Story*? Toys are put on this earth to be played with, that's what they want more than anything else in the world.'"[9]

So he let his sons play with his collection. He did not worry so much about the toys being ruined. This experience gave him a plot idea, about a collector who steals Woody just to display him.

More Ideas from Life

An important theme in *Cars* was also inspired by a real incident. In 2001, Lasseter knew he wanted to make a movie about cars, but he did not have a strong story or a theme. Then he took a two-month road trip across the country with his family.

It was Lasseter's first chance in years to spend so much time with his five sons, Joey, Bennett, P.J., Sam, and Jackson. During the trip, he just lived day-to-day. He had no special plans except to cross the country slowly and have fun with his family.

Lasseter says he learned something important from that trip: The journey of life is its own reward. In other words, sometimes it is good just to slow down and enjoy life without having a special goal. This idea became a big part of *Cars*.

Sometimes Lasseter's personal life and the themes of his movies are very close. For example, one of his sons has juvenile diabetes, a serious but treatable disease. So the plot of *Finding Nemo*—a parent risks everything to save his child—has special meaning for him. The movie was written before his son got sick, but it is especially close to his heart.

Works Well with Others

For years, Lasseter has been the chief creative force at Pixar. He has a reputation for being brilliant about what will work and what will not. But he has learned that it is important not to dominate the team making a movie.

He says that his basic rule is: The best idea is the one that is used. It does not matter whose idea it is. Furthermore, he encourages people to work together, bouncing ideas off each other. He feels that groups working together can think of wonderful things that people working by themselves would never create.

Lasseter also says that he has learned to avoid some of the ways Hollywood studios typically operate. He remembers the time he was unfairly fired from his job at Disney because he made an executive angry. So he makes sure that the atmosphere at Pixar stays open and honest.

John and Nancy Lasseter pose with three of their five sons in 2006. Lasseter's family life inspires many of his film ideas.

Another lesson he has learned from his years of making movies is that competition can be a good thing if it is done in a healthy and supportive way. He likes the fact that Pixar has several competitors, such as DreamWorks. Lasseter just wants

people to watch good animation, no matter which studio makes it.

Creating a Balance

Lasseter's experiences have clearly taught him the value of effort. His hard work has made him rich and famous, and it has made him an important creative artist. But he has also learned that

Lying back on a couch (foreground), Lasseter (left) and Steve Jobs pose with some of the Pixar work force. The company is known for its excellent work environment.

working hard has to be balanced with slowing down to appreciate life.

This balancing act may be especially hard for Lasseter in the years to come. This is because his career keeps reaching newer and higher levels.

CHAPTER 4

To Infinity— and Beyond!

Pixar has not yet made a failure. Its films have made billions of dollars. Critics call them intelligent, entertaining wonders. And they have deeply influenced a new generation of animators, who are looking to expand animation even further.

All of this has made Lasseter one of the most powerful people in Hollywood. One measure of this is that in 2005 he and Pixar chairman Jobs shared the number one spot in *Premiere* magazine's "Power 50 List." This annual list ranks the most influential people in Hollywood.

Lasseter is flattered by such attention. However, he points out that he is not even the most powerful person in his family—his wife comes first. He says, "When I first started appearing on those 'Most Powerful' lists, I think I was number 35. . . . Nancy looked at the list and said, 'Then I guess I'm number 34.'"[10]

Disney Buys Pixar

Recent events in Lasseter's life have only added to his fame. The most important of these came early in 2006. The Disney Corporation bought Pixar, in a deal that cost Disney a whopping $7.4 billion.

Lasseter remained at Pixar after the sale, but he also moved into a top position at Disney Animation Studios. His title at both

From left, Ed Catmull, Steve Jobs, Disney CEO Robert Iger, and Lasseter share smiles after Disney announces it will buy Pixar for $7.4 billion.

places became chief creative officer. This means that he is in charge of the artistic direction at both places. At the same time, he became principal creative adviser at Walt Disney Imagineering. In this role, he will help design new attractions for Disney's theme parks.

Lasseter was thrilled to step into Walt Disney's shoes. It is where he always felt he should be. He comments, "I do what I do in life because of Walt Disney—his films and his theme park and his characters and his joy in entertaining. The emotional feeling that his creations gave me is something that I want to turn around and give to others."[11]

Being Convinced

Walt Disney Studios had long been the leader in animation. But in the ten years before the deal with Pixar, its output went badly downhill. The quality fell, and its new movies flopped. Among the worst were dull sequels to such classics as *Bambi* and *Cinderella*.

Partly because of this poor track record, Lasseter did not want to rejoin Disney. Also, his earlier experience as a Disney employee had ended badly. He was happy at Pixar, where he had full control of quality.

But a new Disney chief, Robert Iger, convinced him. Iger understood that it was wrong for the company to be interested only in making money quickly, rather than in slowly creating excellent material. So Iger guaranteed Lasseter full artistic control.

The Walt Disney studio complex is now home to Pixar. Disney employees were thrilled when Robert Iger successfully lured Lasseter back into the company.

Lasseter agreed. When the deal was announced, the employees of Disney Animation Studios burst into cheers and applause. For John, it was like a wonderful dream. He was back in Disney's animation department, where he had always wanted to be—but this time he was in charge!

Big Plans

Lasseter has big plans for the future. First and foremost, he wants to rebuild Disney's quality. He also wants to encourage such

Lasseter, clowning here in 2007, is working to rebuild the quality of animated films produced by the Disney studio.

moves as making more short cartoons that can be shown before feature films, something that once was a common practice.

He will also remain active at Pixar. He hopes to oversee a new Pixar release once a year (instead of once every year and a half). Pixar's 800 employees still work in Emeryville, but Lasseter hopes to build a new site for the studio in Glendale, close to Disney headquarters.

Beyond Pixar and Disney, John wants to encourage animation by people whose work he admires. One of these is his friend Hayao Miyazaki, the brilliant Japanese animator behind *Howl's*

Moving Castle and other movies. Lasseter adds that he loves the work of many other talented newcomers. He says the industry is just scratching the surface of what animation can do.

The Wienermobile and Other Fun Stuff

Lasseter currently spends part of each week at Disney's headquarters in Burbank, near Los Angeles. But he and his family still live in Sonoma, near Pixar's campus. The Lasseters are active in the community there. For example, they help sponsor the Sonoma Valley Film Festival. They are also active in a number of charities, including the Juvenile Diabetes Foundation.

Lasseter's increasingly busy schedule does not seem to have changed his manner. By all accounts he remains as casual and friendly as ever. His friend Andrew Stanton comments, "John doesn't really change. People change around him."[12]

As a result, Lasseter is still an enthusiastic kid at heart, finding fun in almost everything. He wears Hawaiian shirts and jeans. He rides the Oscar Mayer Wienermobile, not a limousine, to the Academy Awards ceremonies. He dresses up his Oscars in tiny gowns and tuxedos for Christmas and the Academy Awards. And, of course, he still likes to play with toys.

The Future

In the future, Lasseter plans to keep making films that appeal to everyone. He is often asked if Pixar will ever do a film for adults. He usually replies that it already has. All of Pixar's movies have been for adults, he says. It is just that kids like them too.

Although Pixar has yet to have a failure, Lasseter understands that one is bound to come. In fact, he says, this is a joke around the company. He and others take turns directing projects, and they wonder who will have the first flop. Lasseter jokes that he hopes it will not be him.

In the meantime, he is overseeing several projects there. One is *WALL-E*, which came out in summer 2008. It stars a robot left behind on an abandoned Earth in the future. When another robot shows up from space, little WALL-E falls in love.

Lasseter is also overseeing more movies from Walt Disney Studios. One is *Bolt*, scheduled for release in fall 2008. It is about a dog who stars on TV as a dog with superpowers, and he thinks he really has them.

A Sense of History

Lasseter is excited about these and other future projects. But he also believes that it is important to understand the whole history of animation. For example, he loves early Disney cartoons such as 1928's *Steamboat Willie*, one of the first appearances of Mickey Mouse. And he has faith that such classics as *Dumbo* will still make audiences cry and cheer for years to come.

In short, Lasseter says he wants to look back and look forward at the same time. He loves and appreciates all forms of animation, and he hopes audiences can too. That is his goal at Pixar and Disney. To infinity—and beyond!

NOTES

Introduction: Meet Mr. Pixar

1. Quoted in Brett Schlender, "Pixar's Magic Man." *Fortune*, May 17, 2006.

2. Moira Macdonald, "It's OK Honey: We Can't All Be Pixar." *Seattle Times*, November 2, 2007, p. 21H.

Chapter One: The Early Years

3. Quoted in Schlender. "Pixar's Magic Man."

4. Quoted in Mike Lyons, "Toon Story: John Lasseter's Animated Life," *Animation World*, November 1998.

Chapter Two: Building Pixar

5. Quoted in Schlender. "Pixar's Magic Man."

6. Quoted in Lyons, "Toon Story."

Chapter Three: Lessons from Pixar

7. Quoted in Internet Movie Database, "John Lasseter—Biography." http://imdb.com/name/nm0005124/bio.

8. Quoted in Jonathan Ross, "John Lasseter on. . . ." *Guardian Unlimited*, November 19, 2001.

9. Quoted in Ross, "John Lasseter on. . . ."

Chapter Four: To Infinity—and Beyond!

10. Quoted in Barry Koltnow, "Behind the Wheel: Gearhead and Pixar Chief John Lasseter Gets His Animation Motor

Running Again in 'Cars,'" *Orange County Register*, June 9, 2006.

11. Quoted in Schlender, "Pixar's magic man."

12. Quoted in Laura Holson, "He Runs That Mickey Mouse Outfit." *New York Times*, March 4, 2007.

FOR FURTHER EXPLORATION

Books

John Canemaker, *Paper Dreams: The Art and Artists Of Disney Storyboards*. Anaheim, CA: Disney Editions, 2006. This book traces in detail the development of Disney Animation Studio's storyboarding techniques.

Christopher Finch, *The Art of Disney: From Mickey Mouse to the Magic Kingdoms*. New York: Abrams, 2004. A beautifully illustrated history of Disney's animations and other creations.

Danny Fingeroth, *Backstage at an Animated Series*. Danbury, CT: Children's Press, 2003. This book takes readers on a tour of how an animated series is created.

Don Nardo, *Computer Animation*. Farmington Hills, MI: Lucent Books, 2007. A history of the development of computer animation.

Karen Paik, *To Infinity and Beyond!: The Story of Pixar Animation Studios*. San Francisco: Chronicle, 2007. This history of Pixar was not written for kids, but it has lots of wonderful graphics and a foreword by John Lasseter.

Peggy Parks, *Computer Animator*. Farmington Hills, MI: Kid-Haven, 2005. This book discusses different aspects of becoming a professional computer animator.

Frank Thomas and Ollie Johnston, *The Illusion of Life: Disney Animation*. New York: Hyperion, 1995. The text of this book (by two veteran animators) is not for kids, but the graphics are wonderful.

Walter Foster Publishing, *Learn to Draw Your Favorite Disney/Pixar Characters*. Laguna Hills, CA: Walter Foster, 2005. A book showing step-by-step ways to draw some of Pixar's best-known characters.

Web Sites

BrainPop.com Digital Animation (www.brainpop.com/artsand music/artconcepts/digitalanimation/preview.weml). This site is part of the popular BrainPop science site for kids.

Disney.com Characters (http://home.disney.go.com/characters/ index). Disney's official site has plenty to see and do, including games, trailers, and information about Pixar releases.

National Gallery of Art: Flip Book and Computer Animation (www.nga.gov/kids/stella/activityflip.htm). This Web site shows how kids can create simple computer animation on their own.

Pixar Animation Studios (www.pixar.com/). This official site has lots of great stuff, including sneak peeks of shorts.

INDEX

PICTURE CREDITS

About the Author

Adam Woog has written many books for adults, young readers, and children. He has a special interest in history, biography, music, and the movies. Woog lives with his wife and daughter in Seattle, Washington.